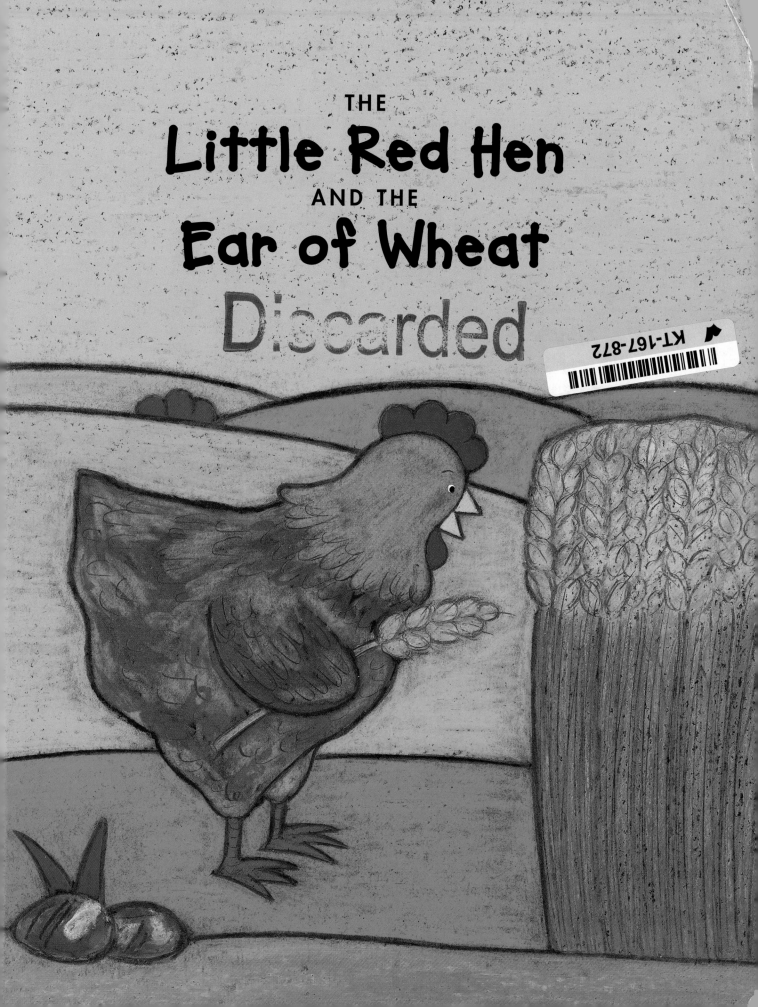

THE
Little Red Hen
AND THE
Ear of Wheat

For my mother — M. F.
For Chris, Céline, Fiona and Dominique — E. B.

Barefoot Books
124 Walcot Street
Bath
BA1 5BG

Hardcover ISBN 1 902283 33 3
Paperback ISBN 1 902283 34 1

Graphic design by Jennie Hoare, Bradford on Avon
Colour separation by Unifoto, Cape Town
Printed and bound in China

British Library Cataloguing-in-Publication Data: a catalogue
record for this book is available from the British Library.

7 9 8

THE
Little Red Hen
AND THE
Ear of Wheat

written by MARY FINCH • illustrated by ELISABETH BELL

Barefoot Books
Celebrating Art and Story

Once upon a time
a cock and a mouse
and a little red hen
lived together in a
small brown house
with a red roof.

One day the little red hen
found a grain of wheat
lying on the ground.
'Look what I've found,'
she said to the cock
and the mouse.

'I shall plant it in the earth.
Who will help me?'
'Not I,' said the cock.
'Not I,' said the mouse.
'Then I'll do it myself,'
said the little red hen.

She scratched at the earth
and planted the grain.
'Who will help me water it?'
'Not I,' said the cock.
'Not I,' said the mouse.
'Then I'll do it myself,'
said the little red hen.

She watered the earth and waited for the wheat to grow. The sun shone, and the wheat grew tall and straight.

When the ear of wheat
was golden, she said:
'Who will help me harvest it?'
'Not I,' said the cock.
'Not I,' said the mouse.
'Then I'll do it myself,'
said the little red hen.

She picked the ear of wheat
and put it in a basket.
'Who will help me take it to
the mill to be ground into flour?'

'Not I,' said the cock.
'Not I,' said the mouse.
'Then I'll do it myself,'
said the little red hen.

The miller ground the ear of wheat into fine white flour. 'Who will help me make this flour into dough?'

'Not I,' said the cock.
'Not I,' said the mouse.
'Then I'll do it myself,'
said the little red hen.

She mixed the flour into warm, yeasty dough. 'Who will help me knead this dough into bread?'

'Not I,' said the cock.
'Not I,' said the mouse.
'Then I'll do it myself,'
said the little red hen.

She made the dough
into a round, shiny loaf.
'Who will help me put
this loaf into the oven?'

'Not I,' said the cock.
'Not I,' said the mouse.
'Then I'll do it myself,'
said the little red hen.

She put the loaf into
the oven to bake.
When it was ready,
she took out the
brown, crusty loaf.

'Who will help me eat
this warm fresh bread?'
'I will,' said the cock.
'I will,' said the mouse.

'No, you won't,'
said the little red hen.
'I shall eat it myself,'
said the little red hen.
And she did.

'Oh,' said the cock.
'Oh,' said the mouse.
'You didn't help me,'
said the little red hen.
'So I ate it myself,'
said the little red hen.

But the next time the little red hen found a grain of wheat lying on the ground,

the cock scratched
at the earth and
planted the grain,

the mouse
watered
the earth,

and together the cock
and the mouse and
the little red hen
watched the wheat
grow tall and straight.

Together they took the wheat
to the mill to be ground, and
together they made the flour
into dough.

And when the dough was cooked, the cock and the mouse and the little red hen sat down together and ate the nice, warm bread — and it was delicious!

HOW TO BAKE A WHEATMEAL COB

It is easy to bake your own bread. Homemade bread smells wonderful and tastes delicious. To make a wheatmeal cob like the little red hen's, you will need:

Ingredients
1 lb (480 g) wheatmeal flour
2 level teaspoonfuls salt
2 level teaspoonfuls sugar
a knob of lard
1/2oz (15 g) fresh yeast
1/2pt (300 ml) tepid water

Equipment
a sieve
a large mixing bowl
a small mixing bowl
a saucepan or kettle
a pint measuring jug
a wooden spoon
a teaspoon
a tablespoon
a tea-towel
a metal baking sheet
a small, sharp knife

Method

1. Before you start, have all your ingredients and equipment ready. Bread rises best in a warm, draught-free room, so make sure that the mixing bowls are warm and that you have warm hands.

2. Sift the flour, salt and sugar through the sieve into the large mixing bowl.

3. Rub in the lard with your fingertips.

4. Put the yeast into the small mixing bowl. Heat the water in a saucepan or kettle until it is tepid; it must not be too hot. Pour about two tablespoons of water on to the yeast, then blend the yeast and water together with a teaspoon. Leave the mixture for five minutes. After this time it should start to bubble; this shows that the yeast is alive. Now stir in the rest of the water.

5. Make a well in the middle of the flour and stir in the water and yeast mixture with a wooden spoon. Then use your hands to work the mixture into a soft dough that leaves the sides of the bowl clean. If your hands get very sticky dip them in some more flour.

6. Turn the dough on to a floured surface and knead it for about ten minutes until it is smooth and elastic.

7. Shape the dough into a round loaf and place it on a lightly greased metal baking sheet. Use the knife to cut a slit or a cross on the top of the loaf.

8. Cover the loaf with a tea-towel and leave it in a warm place, such as the airing cupboard or the top of the cooker, for about forty minutes until it has doubled in size. While you are waiting for it to rise, preheat the oven to 230° C (450° F, Gas Mark 8). The oven will get very hot so make sure that you have a grown-up with you before you open it. To test that the loaf is ready to bake, press it lightly with a floured finger. If it springs back into shape, it is ready. Brush the top of the loaf lightly with a little milk or water.

9. Bake the loaf for about 30-40 minutes until it is well risen and a rich brown. To check if it is cooked, tap the bottom of it with your knuckles (be careful — it will be hot). It should sound hollow if it is ready. Remove the loaf from the baking sheet and leave to cool on a wire rack.

Michael Bond

Favourite Paddington Stories

Paddington
in the
Garden

Paddington
at the
Carnival

Paddington
and the
Grand Tour

Illustrated by R. W. Alley

This collection first published in paperback in Great Britain by HarperCollins Children's Books in 2014

Paddington in the Garden first published in hardback by HarperCollins Publishers, USA, in 2002
First published in hardback in Great Britain by HarperCollins Publishers in 2002
First published in paperback by HarperCollins Children's Books in 2008

Paddington at the Carnival first published in hardback by HarperCollins Publishers, USA, in 1997
First published in hardback in Great Britain by Collins in 1998
First published in paperback by Picture Lions in 2007
Revised paperback edition published by HarperCollins Children's Books in 2009

Paddington and the Grand Tour first published in hardback and paperback in Great Britain by HarperCollins Publishers Ltd in 2003
Revised paperback edition published by HarperCollins Children's Books in 2008

1 3 5 7 9 10 8 6 4 2

Collins and Picture Lions are imprints of HarperCollins Children's Books.
HarperCollins Children's Books is a division of HarperCollins Publishers Ltd.

ISBN: 978-0-00-758010-1

Text copyright © Michael Bond 1997, 2002, 2003, 2008
Illustrations copyright © R. W. Alley 1997, 2002, 2003

Visit our website at: www.harpercollins.co.uk

Printed in China